Roald Dahl's Fantabulous Facts

KT-405-879

There's loads of fun to be had the whole year round in this little book, jam-packed with letters and observations by Roald Dahl himself. Plus there are plenty of weird and wonderful facts, jokes, puzzles and the odd scrumdiddlyumptious recipe thrown in for good measure!

This book has been specially published for World Book Day 2012.

For further information please see **www.worldbookday.com**

World Book Day in the UK and Ireland is made possible by generous sponsorship from National Book Tokens, participating publishers, authors and booksellers.

Booksellers who accept the £1 World Book Day Token bear the full cost of redeeming it.

04745959

Discover the Gloriumptious World of Roald Dahl

Also available on Puffin Audio

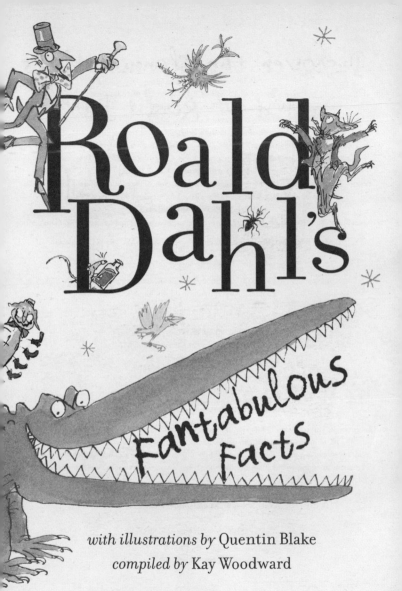

Roald Dahl's
Fantabulous Facts

with illustrations by Quentin Blake
compiled by Kay Woodward

PUFFIN

PUFFIN BOOKS

Published by the Penguin Group

Penguin Books Ltd, 80 Strand, London WC2R 0RL, England

Penguin Group (USA) Inc., 375 Hudson Street, New York, New York 10014, USA

Penguin Group (Canada), 90 Eglinton Avenue East, Suite 700, Toronto, Ontario, Canada M4P 2Y3
(a division of Pearson Penguin Canada Inc.)

Penguin Ireland, 25 St Stephen's Green, Dublin 2, Ireland (a division of Penguin Books Ltd)

Penguin Group (Australia), 250 Camberwell Road, Camberwell, Victoria 3124, Australia
(a division of Pearson Australia Group Pty Ltd)

Penguin Books India Pvt Ltd, 11 Community Centre, Panchsheel Park, New Delhi – 110 017, India

Penguin Group (NZ), 67 Apollo Drive, Rosedale, Auckland 0632, New Zealand
(a division of Pearson New Zealand Ltd)

Penguin Books (South Africa) (Pty) Ltd, 24 Sturdee Avenue, Rosebank, Johannesburg 2196, South Africa

Penguin Books Ltd, Registered Offices: 80 Strand, London WC2R 0RL, England

puffinbooks.com

Originally published as *The Dahlmanac* 2006
Published with revisions in this edition 2012

001 – 10 9 8 7 6 5 4 3 2 1

Text copyright © Roald Dahl Nominee Ltd, 2012
Illustrations copyright © Quentin Blake, 2012
All rights reserved

The moral right of the author and illustrator has been asserted

Text design by Mandy Norman

Printed in Great Britain by Clays Ltd, St Ives plc

British Library Cataloguing in Publication Data
A CIP catalogue record for this book is available from the British Library

ISBN: 978-0-141-34230-6

www.greenpenguin.co.uk

MIX
Paper from
responsible sources
FSC www.fsc.org   FSC™ C018179

Penguin Books is committed to a sustainable
future for our business, our readers and our
planet. This book is made from paper certified
by the Forest Stewardship Council.

September

Roald Dahl went to boarding school when he was nine. He wrote to his mother once a week without fail, and she kept all his letters! As you can see, young Roald's spelling was awful.

Probably Dahl family pets

Dear Mama

    I am sorry I have not writting before. I hope none of you have got coalds. IT is quite a nice day To-day, I am just going To church. I hope (mike) is quite all right now, and (Buzz.) Major Cottam is goingTo recite som*Thing caled ("as you like it") To night. plese could you send me some (conkers) as quick as you can, but ~~do not~~ dont send To meny , ~~the~~ just send them in a Tin and wrapit up in paper

See page 12

Love from
BOY

A play by Shakespeare

Young Roald sometimes signed his letters like this.

Happy birthday, Roald!

Roald Dahl was born on 13 September 1916.

Other famous people born in the same month include:

☆ Beyoncé Knowles (singer and actor)
  4 September 1981

☆ Queen Elizabeth I (the famous Tudor queen)
  7 September 1533

☆ Prince Harry (royal prince)
  15 September 1984

☆ Agatha Christie (deadly crime author)
  15 September 1890

☆ George Cadbury (real chocolate-factory owner)
  19 September 1839

☆ T.S. Eliot (poet)
  26 September 1888

☆ Serena Williams (whizzy tennis player)
  26 September 1981

☆ Gwyneth Paltrow (actor)
  27 September 1972

Did you know?

13 September is the 256th day of the year, apart from leap years when it's the 257th day.

True or false?

Every year, Roald Dahl had an enormous, gooey, squidgy, sticky chocolate sponge cake for his birthday – just like the one that Bruce Bogtrotter ate in *Matilda*.

False

Although Roald loved chocolate, he was not fond of chocolate-flavoured food – including chocolate cake.

3

How to Say 'Happy birthday' in 11 different languages

Hartelijk gefeliciteerd!
Dutch

Joyeux anniversaire!
French

Janam din ki badhai!
Hindi

Hau`oli la hanau!
Hawaiian

Til hamingju med afmaelisdaginn!
Icelandic

Gratulerer med dagen!
Norwegian

Suk san wan keut!
Thai

Buon compleanno!
Italian

Penblwydd hapus i chi!
Welsh

Yom Holedet Sameach!
Hebrew

Feliz cumpleaños!
Spanish

Roald Dahl says...

'Hunting for wild field-mushrooms is truly one of my favourite pastimes. Mushrooms are very mysterious things. They will grow in one field but not in another and there is no explanation for it. But to walk slowly across a green field in the autumn and spot suddenly ahead of you that little pure white dome nestling in the grass, that, I tell you, is exciting.'

Mushrooms that can KILL you!

Fly Agaric – the classic red mushroom with white spots that you see in fairy stories

Devil's Bolete – creamy white and smells unpleasant

Deadly Galerina – dark brown and slimy

Death Cap – yellowish green and smells sickly sweet

Destroying Angel – white, but smells sickly sweet

Q: Why did the mushroom go to the party?
A: *Because he was a fungi.*

How to tell a mushroom from a toadstool

– some things to look out for:

Mushrooms usually grow in open fields, not under trees or shrubs like toadstools.

The upper part of a mushroom – the cap – should be white and smooth with no scales or warts. Toadstools will often have a different coloured cap with scales and raised lumps on it.

The cap of a true mushroom pulls away from the stem as it grows, which leaves a ring of tissue round the stem. If you can't find a ring of tissue, it's not a true mushroom.

The undersurface of both mushroom and toadstool caps has gills. In a young mushroom these are pink, but they turn brown to almost black as the mushroom matures. Toadstools or poisonous mushrooms have gills that remain white throughout their entire life cycle.

MUSHROOM

cap

gills

ring of tissue

base of stem

TOADSTOOL

cap

gills

stalk

base of stem

WARNING

Do NOT eat any mushrooms or toadstools that you find in the wild as many of them can be highly poisonous. Get them checked by an expert first.

POISON

Roald Dahl Day

13 September

Even though Roald Dahl is no longer around, his fans plan to celebrate his birthday. One way is to do the Roald Dahl Challenge: ten fun activities inspired by Roald Dahl himself.

1. Wear something yellow – it was his favourite colour.

2. Wear one or more items of clothing backwards.

3. Gobblefunk! (In other words, use the unique language created by Roald Dahl and spoken by the BFG.)

4. Swap a Roald Dahl book with a friend.

5. Talk backwards. Ysae os reve s'ti!

6. Tell a silly joke – Roald Dahl loved swapping these with his children.

7. Play an unexpected prank.

8. Give someone a treat – Roald was a great believer in treats, whether it was a bar of chocolate or a lovely surprise.

9. Write your own revolting rhyme.

10. Make up an Oompa-Loompa dance and get all your friends to join in.

How to play conkers

A conker is a hard, shiny, dark-brown nut that falls from the horse-chestnut tree at this time of year. Conkers is a game of accuracy and skill, in which players take it in turns to hit each other's conkers.

What you need:

- ☆ Two players
- ☆ Two lengths of string
- ☆ Two conkers

What you do:

1. Each player makes a hole in their conker with a skewer, then threads it on to a piece of string, knotting it securely.

2. The **first player** wraps the end of the string round their hand, allowing the conker to hang down. It must be perfectly still.

3. **The opponent** – known as **the striker** – also wraps the end of the string round their hand, then pulls back the conker with the other hand before attempting to strike the hanging conker.

4. If the striker misses, they are allowed two more shots.

5. If the strings tangle, the first player to shout **'Strings!'** gets another go.

6. And if a conker falls to the ground it's perfectly legal for the striker to shout **'Stamps!'** and stamp on it as hard as they can – unless the conker's owner gets in first with **'No stamps!'**

7. The conker players take turns at being the striker until one of the conkers is destroyed.

How to Score:

☆ Every conker is given a number.

☆ A brand-new conker is called Conker 1.

☆ A conker that has beaten another brand-new conker is Conker 2.

☆ A conker that has beaten five brand-new conkers is Conker 6.

☆ But if this Conker 6 beats a Conker 3 then it would become Conker 10. One point is added for the conker victory, plus another three points for the beaten conker's previous score.

Back to school

Q: Why did the teacher put the lights on?

A: Because the class was so dim.

Q: Did you hear about the cross-eyed teacher?

A: He couldn't control his pupils.

October

Roald Dahl's
youngest sister →

St. Peter's
Weston-Super-mare

Dear (Asta,)

Thanks awfully for your letter and the comb. When your rabbits were shot, did'nt Lena hear the shooting, if you get some more I don't suppose you'll ~~leave~~ put them in the same place.

Will you remind Mama not to forget the (roler)-skates, (a man's pair)

I expect as you read this you will either be sucking your thum in Mama's bed, or you will be in your own, with (Else) leaning over you, and saying "Let's see".

Well, Dont forget to tell Mama about the ROLER skates.

Another younger sister

love from

Roald

See
page
22

15

Roald Dahl says...

'This, like September, is a lovely month, mild and misty and smelling of ripe apples. We have a small orchard of about five acres at the back of our house and when I first came here nearly forty years ago there were seventy huge old fruit-trees filling the whole field. There were apples, pears, cherries and plums and all of them must have been there since the last century. There was so much fruit every autumn that I told all the children in the village they could come in at any time and ask to borrow a ladder and pick what they wanted. They came in droves.'

Bobbing for apples

This is one of the oldest and most traditional Halloween games.

All you need is:

- ☆ A large bowl
- ☆ Water
- ☆ Apples
- ☆ A pair of teeth, preferably your own

Fill a bowl with water and throw in a few apples. Then put your hands behind your back and try to pick up an apple using only your teeth.

WARNING
You might get seriously wet.

Halloween

Halloween takes place on 31 October.
It's the scariest night of the year,
when spirits and spooks and
ghouls walk among us.
This makes it the perfect time
to read Roald Dahl's *The Witches*.
That's if you dare, of course.

Did you know?

Halloween is short for
ALL HALLOW EVEN
(hallow means 'holy') so called
because it's the night before
All Saints' Day.

MOST HAUNTED PLACES IN THE BRITISH ISLES

THE TOWER OF LONDON, ENGLAND – once a prison and a place where royal prisoners were executed, so it's no wonder ghosts have been seen here. The most famous are Anne Boleyn, the second wife of King Henry VIII, and the Princes in the Tower (two little boys walking hand in hand). Many of the ghosts – including a troop of soldiers and a bear – have been seen standing at different tower windows or walking through walls.

BORLEY RECTORY, ESSEX, ENGLAND – once known as the most haunted house in England, there were phantom footsteps, spooky whispers and eerie lights. A ghostly nun was a frequent visitor too.

BALGONIE CASTLE, FIFE, SCOTLAND – Green Jeannie (so called because she is said to be a fetching shade of green) wanders around Scotland's most haunted castle in the small hours of the morning.

THE PROMENADE, PRESTATYN, WALES – keep a lookout for the White Lady of Prestatyn, who is often seen taking a twilight stroll beside the seaside.

KILLAKEE HOUSE, CO DUBLIN, IRELAND – the Black Cat of Killakee once haunted this place, its blazing red eyes terrifying anyone unlucky enough to cross its path ...

10 ways to spot REAL WITCHES

– according to Roald Dahl

1. They are always women.

2. Instead of fingernails, they have thin curvy claws, like a cat.

3. They wear gloves all the time – except when they are in bed.

4. They are bald.

5. They wear first-class wigs ...

6. ... and those wigs set up a frightful itch on their bald scalps.

7. They have slightly larger nose-holes than ordinary people ...

8. ... for smelling children with.

9. They have no toes.

10. They have blue spit.

Did you know?

In the seventeenth century, just after the Civil War, people in the UK were convinced witches really existed. Men were actually employed to ride around the country, sniffing out witches and sending them for trial. The chief of these was called **Matthew Hopkins**. He was known as the

WITCHFINDER GENERAL.

2 OF THE MOST COMMON TESTS FOR WITCHES

Witchmarks: unusual moles, birthmarks or warts were thought to be Devil's Marks and, if poked with a pin, would not bleed or cause pain. Matthew Hopkins had a 'jabbing needle' with a 7.5cm-long spike which retracted into the spring-loaded handle. Not surprisingly, he found a lot of witches!

The water test: an accused witch had her thumbs tied to her opposite big toes (left hand to right foot) and was flung into the river or a handy pond. If she floated she was guilty; if she sank she was innocent. So she lost either way!

Back in time

At 1 a.m. precisely on the last Sunday of October, the clocks go back an hour. British Summer Time is officially over. But there is a bonus – you get a whole extra hour. Here are some suggestions for things to do in it:

☆ Learn to rollerskate.

☆ Dive into a book – not your favourite, most well-thumbed one but one that you've *never* read before.

☆ Practise saying 'happy birthday' in different languages (see pages 4–5).

☆ Learn to juggle. Start with two balls and move on to three.

'Spring forward, fall back'

A cunning phrase to remind you which way the clocks move in spring and in autumn. In spring, the clocks spring forward an hour. In fall (the American way of saying autumn – because the leaves fall off the trees), the clocks fall back an hour.

Greenwich Mean Time

Wherever you are in the world, all time is measured against the time at Greenwich in London. For example, the time in Hong Kong, China, is said to be 8 hours ahead of Greenwich Mean Time (GMT). New York City, USA, is 5 hours behind GMT. At twelve noon precisely in Greenwich and the rest of the UK, tell the time around the world with this handy timetable:

2 a.m.
Honolulu, Hawaii, USA

4 a.m.
San Francisco, USA

6 a.m.
Mexico City, Mexico

7 a.m.
Québec, Canada

9 a.m.
Buenos Aires, Argentina

12 noon
London, UK

1 p.m.
Berlin, Germany

2 p.m.
Cairo, Egypt

3 p.m.
Moscow, Russia

3.30 p.m.
Tehran, Iran

5.30 p.m.
Mumbai, India

8 p.m.
Beijing, China

10 p.m.
Sydney, Australia

Q: What do the Oompa-Loompas celebrate on 31 October?
A: *Marshmalloween!*

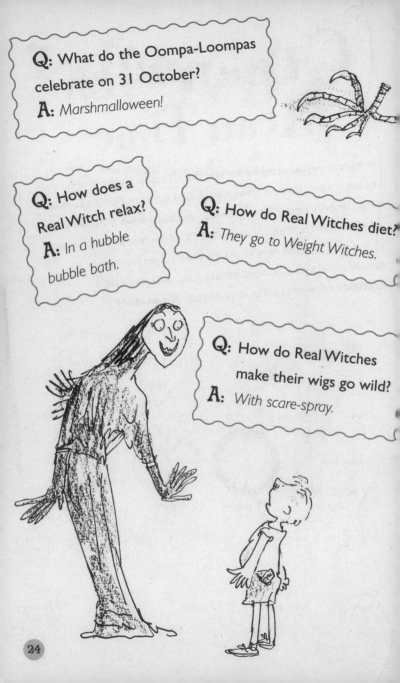

Q: How does a Real Witch relax?
A: *In a hubble bubble bath.*

Q: How do Real Witches diet?
A: *They go to Weight Witches.*

Q: How do Real Witches make their wigs go wild?
A: *With scare-spray.*

November

Time for fireworks and Bonfire Night!

November 8th 1925

No I

St Peters
Weston-super-mare

Dear Mama

Thank you for your letter. We had a lovely time on thursday, that ½ Mount veuvius was the prettyest I had first it made a gold fountain and then a silver one, and we had big bonfire with a guy on top, and another of the prettyest of my fireworks was the snow storm, it lit up the hole place.

See page 26

See page 27

The Gunpowder Plot

REMEMBER, REMEMBER THE FIFTH OF NOVEMBER, GUNPOWDER, TREASON AND PLOT; I SEE NO REASON WHY GUNPOWDER TREASON SHOULD EVER BE FORGOT.

On **5 November 1605**, Guy Fawkes and twelve other conspirators tried to blow up the Houses of Parliament. Thirty-six barrels of gunpowder were hidden in cellars beneath Parliament, but at the last minute some of the plotters began to have second thoughts. One even sent a letter to an MP friend, warning him to stay at home on 5 November. The letter reached the attention of the king and the gunpowder was discovered – and Guy Fawkes with it. That night, bonfires were lit around the country to celebrate the plot's failure. Guy Fawkes was not burnt on a bonfire like the stuffed guys nowadays but was instead hanged, drawn and quartered – a very nasty end.

Roald Dahl says...

'Oh, how we used to look forward to the fifth of November at boarding school. In these enlightened times, no one will believe the things we were allowed to do on that famous night . . . boys from seven to twelve years old all setting off their own fireworks with their own matches. Pretty lethal fireworks too.'

WE FORK SIR*

Can you unscramble the names of Roald Dahl's favourite fireworks?

☆ A CALM DR NEON

☆ CO TREK

☆ BRACKEN CRAG

☆ A NERD LOG IN

☆ REPENT FIRES

Answers on page 118

* FIREWORKS, of course!

27

10 things you might not know about VOLCANOES

For real explosions, check out these volcanic facts:

1. When a volcano erupts, it can shoot ash as far as 40km into the air.

2. The biggest volcano in the world is Mauna Loa in Hawaii. It is over 8km high, though some of it is underwater.

3. The most active volcano in the world is Kilauea in Hawaii. It has been erupting almost non-stop since 1983.

4. Roald Dahl's screenplay for the 1967 James Bond film, *You Only Live Twice*, included a top-secret hideaway inside a volcano, complete with an evil baddy and a monorail.

5. There are at least 1,500 volcanoes on Earth. About 150 volcanoes erupt every year.

6. When Vesuvius – Italy's most famous volcano – erupted in AD 79, it buried the nearby towns of Herculaneum and Pompeii under tonnes of ash.

7. The area around the Pacific Ocean where earthquakes and volcanic eruptions are common is called the Ring of Fire.

8. A volcanic eruption usually lasts between ten and 100 days.

9. When Mount St Helens, Washington, erupted in 1980, it was one of the USA's biggest volcanic explosions ever.

10. When the Eyjafjallajökull volcano, one of Iceland's largest, erupted in 2010, it sent clouds of ash as high as 11,000 metres, disrupting air traffic and stranding thousands of passengers for weeks.

Recipe for Savoury Crocodile

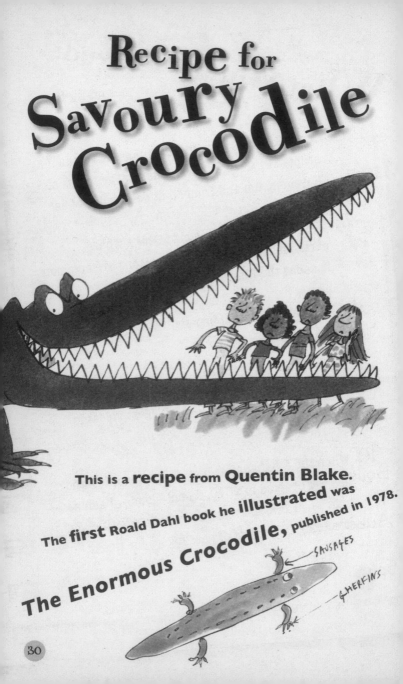

This is a **recipe** from **Quentin Blake**.

The **first** Roald Dahl book he **illustrated** was

The Enormous Crocodile, published in 1978.

SAUSAGES

GHERKINS

What you will need:

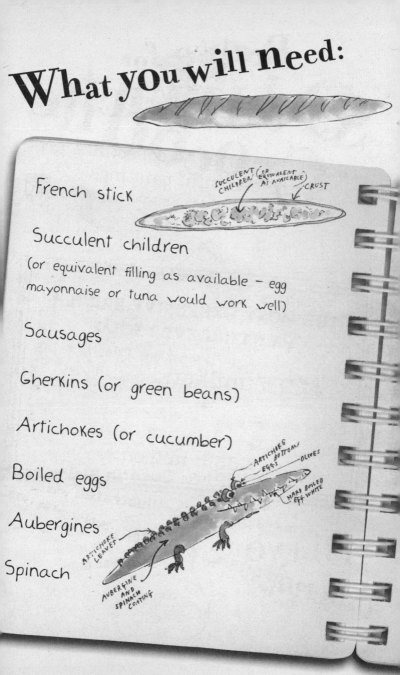

French stick

Succulent children

(or equivalent filling as available — egg mayonnaise or tuna would work well)

Sausages

Gherkins (or green beans)

Artichokes (or cucumber)

Boiled eggs

Aubergines

Spinach

SUCCULENT CHILDREN (OR EQUIVALENT AS AVAILABLE)

CRUST

ARTICHOKE EGGS BOTTOMS

OLIVES

HARD BOILED EGG WHITE

ARTICHOKE LEAVES

AUBERGINE AND SPINACH COATING

Odd _{arty} facts

Roald Dahl loved to collect fine art and beautiful paintings.
Here are some odd facts that might have intrigued him.

THE MOST EXPENSIVE BRITISH PAINTING EVER SOLD

In July 2007, a painting of Rome by J. M. W. Turner was sold for

£29.7 million at Sotheby's, London.

The most expensive painting ever is Picasso's *Nude, Green Leaves and Bust*, sold in New York in 2010 for

£65.5 million.

Did you know?

In **1888** the famous painter **Vincent Van Gogh** (he painted *Sunflowers*) cut off part of his left ear and gave it to someone as a present.

THE MOST FAMOUS PAINTING IN THE WORLD

The **Mona Lisa** by **Leonardo da Vinci** is generally considered to be the most famous painting in the history of art. It was painted between **1503** and **1505** and is a portrait of a real woman, Monna (or Mona) Lisa, who was married to Francesco del Giacondo – which explains the other name of the painting: *La Giaconda*. In 2004, the painting was valued at over $608 million! However, many people consider it to be priceless.

The man who stole the *Mona Lisa*

On **21 August 1911**, the *Mona Lisa* was stolen from the **Louvre museum** in Paris. The police searched the museum from top to bottom (which took a week because it is so large) but the only thing they found was the heavy frame. Two years later, the thief was identified when an Italian called **Vincenzo Perugia** tried to sell the painting to the **Uffizi Gallery** in Florence for **$100,000**. Apparently he had hidden overnight in the Louvre, then, when the museum was closed, had unhooked the painting from the wall and cut it out of its frame. While trying to leave the building, he came to a locked door. He simply unscrewed the doorknob, put it in his pocket and walked outside with the world's most famous painting under his jacket.

A sad day

Roald Dahl died on **23 November 1990** at the age of seventy-four. The last two books he wrote were published after his death. They were *The Vicar of Nibbleswicke* and *The Minpins*.

Did you know?

Roald Dahl thought the best book he ever wrote was *The BFG*. Do you agree?

December

Dec. 12ᵗʰ 1926.

Dear Mama,

This is my last letter to you this term. We had a special treat last night, we all hung up our stockings, and when it was dark matron came in dressed up as (father xmas) and put things in our stockings, I got a kind of a musical ~ and a soldier on a horse in mine. the same night ~ hung up hers outside her door and we all put ~gs in it, it was full in the end. We start Excams ~est Tuesday and they go on till to Thursday.
AM COMING HOME NEXT FRIDAY

See page 40

35

Happy birthday Quentin!

Quentin Blake was born on 16 December 1932 in Sidcup, Kent. His first drawing was published when he was just sixteen and he went on to illustrate a huge number of children's books – including all but one of Roald Dahl's (The Minpins is the exception). He has also written and illustrated many of his own titles.

10 things you might not know about Quentin Blake

1. He started drawing when he was five years old.

2. He liked school and once learnt to be a teacher. (He's actually a proper professor.)

3. When he is drawing someone's expression he pulls the same face himself.

4. He was nervous about first meeting Roald Dahl, but they soon became the best of friends.

5. Quentin draws lots of roughs before completing his final drawing.

6. His favourite Roald Dahl book is *The BFG*.

7. Of his own books, he likes *Clown* best.

8. Roald Dahl once sent Quentin a sandal through the post to show him what the BFG's footwear should look like.

9. In 1999 Quentin became the very first Children's Laureate and spent the next two years doing everything he could to promote children's literature.

10. Roald Dahl called him Quent.

To find out even more about the fantastic Quentin Blake, visit his website:

quentinblake.com

What Roald Dahl thought about Christmas

Roald Dahl loved giving presents, but he hated Christmas. Here's what he thought about it:

1. Christmas is for children.

2. Grown-ups should try to make Christmas fun for children.

3. Christmas is a bonanza for shopkeepers. Everyone else gets poor.

4. Home-made Christmas cards are the best things ever.

5. Christmas cards with photos of the senders on the front are the worst things ever.

6. Presents should be given to family members and no one else.

7. Goose tastes wonderful . . .

8. . . . but turkey is one of the most tasteless meats that it is possible to find.

9. The best presents of all are the simplest ones.

10. One of Roald Dahl's favourite presents was a glass jar of wine gums given to him by his daughter Ophelia.

Top 10 Christmas firsts

1. The first **Christmas card** was sent in the UK in **1843**.

2. The first **charity Christmas card** was sent in **1949** – all profits went to UNICEF (the United Nations Children's Fund).

3. The picture of **Father Christmas** as we know him today – a jolly round man in a red-and-white suit – first appeared in a **1931** Coca-Cola advert drawn by Haddon Sundblom. Before then, the Victorians had shown him wearing red, blue, green or brown. In the US, he had worn red, but he had been an elf, not a human. If you've seen him, you'll know of course what he looks like!

4. The first **Christmas cracker** was pulled in **1846**.

5. The first **advent calendar** was made in Germany in **1851** . . .

6. . . . but the first **chocolate-filled advent calendar** wasn't produced until a whole century later!

7. In **1834**, Prince Albert – Queen Victoria's husband – introduced the first **Christmas tree** to Windsor Castle. Soon, the rest of the UK joined in.

8. The first **Christmas fairy lights** appeared just three years after Thomas Edison invented the light bulb. One of the American inventor's friends – Edward Johnson – used them to decorate his tree in **1882**.

9. **Tinsel** was invented in Germany in **1610**. The first garland was made of real silver.

10. The first **English collection of carols** was published in **1521**, but they were probably sung much earlier than that.

What was in Roald Dahl's cellar?

Cases and cases of wine!

Roald Dahl loved wine, and his large cellar, with a constant temperature of 12.8°C, summer and winter, was an ideal storing place. Some years are better than others as far as wine-making is concerned. **1982** was a very good year for wine and Roald bought 1,000 cases (with 12 bottles in a case, that's a great party!). Then, because the way down to his cellar was long and steep, he had to have a wooden chute made so that he could slide the cases into place rather than carry them.

Other really good years for wine were:

1959, 1961, 1990, 2000, 2005, 2009.

Did you know?

Conventional wine is made from grapes, but you can make wine from practically anything, including parsnips, beetroot, dandelions, carrots and potatoes. Anyone for a glass of swede?

January

See page 48

St. Peter's,
Weston-super-mare.
January 27th, 1926.

Asta, Roald's
youngest sister

Dear Baby

We had a fine game of ruggar yesterday, I was one of
the captain's, they beat us 24 21 points to 1, but we had all the
little ones smaller boys on our side excepetone or two, we got awful-
ey dirty we got splashed all over with mud, to day we go for
a run, you see we go run about three 1½ miles and then run back, we
do that once a week to get pratés but we'r awfuly stiff the
next morning.

43

Roald Dahl says...

'As the clock approaches midnight on the thirty-first of December you are still in the old year, but then all at once, one millionth of a second after midnight, you are in the new . . . The same sort of thing happens on your birthday when you are nine years old one day and ten years old the next. It is lovely to be a year older, but it is the suddenness of it all that is so amazing.'

New Year's resolutions:

Can you guess which of Roald Dahl's characters might have made these New Year's resolutions?

1. 'To repair the chocolate-factory roof.'

2. 'To read *Encyclopaedia Britannica*. All of it.'

3. 'To win first prize in a giant fruit and vegetable competition.'

4. '*Not* to eat cabbage soup – not this year, not next year, not ever again!'

5. 'To inspect spaghetti suppers very thoroughly before a single strand passes my lips.'

Answers on page 118

How did the months get their names?

January – named after Janus, the two-faced Roman god who looked backwards and forwards

February – named after the Roman feast, *februa*, always held in this month

March – once the first month of the Roman year, it was named after Mars, the god of war

April – from the Latin word *aperire*, meaning 'to open'. It is traditionally a month of new growth, when buds open and plants come to life after winter

May – named after Maia, the goddess of growth

June – named after Juno, the goddess of young women

July – named in honour of Julius Caesar, a famous Roman general who conquered Britain. He was later stabbed to death

August – named after another Roman general, this time Caesar Augustus

September – from the Latin *septum*, which means 'seven'. Even though September is the ninth month of the year, it used to be the seventh month of the Roman calendar

October – from the Latin *octo*, which means 'eight', because it used to be the eighth month of the Roman year

November – from the Latin *novem*, which means 'nine'

December – from the Latin *decem*, which means 'ten'

Roald Dahl
and the dragon!

According to the Chinese calendar, each year is named after a different animal – twelve animals in all. Roald Dahl was born in the Year of the Dragon. Which year were you and other members of your family born in?

Year of the Rat
1948, 1960, 1972, 1984, 1996, 2008

Year of the Ox
1949, 1961, 1973, 1985, 1997, 2009

Year of the Tiger
1950, 1962, 1974, 1986, 1998, 2010

Year of the Hare
1951, 1963, 1975, 1987, 1999, 2011

Year of the Dragon
1952, 1964, 1976, 1988, 2000, 2012

Year of the Snake
1953, 1965, 1977, 1989, 2001

Year of the Horse
1954, 1966, 1978, 1990, 2002

Year of the Sheep
1955, 1967, 1979, 1991, 2003

Year of the Monkey
1956, 1968, 1980, 1992, 2004

Year of the Rooster
1957, 1969, 1981, 1993, 2005

Year of the Dog
1958, 1970, 1982, 1994, 2006

Year of the Pig
1959, 1971, 1983, 1995, 2007

③ Sports that Roald Dahl enjoyed

At school young Roald played sports all year round, even in freezing cold January. It was fortunate that he was good at sport and even more fortunate that he liked it. Here are some of his favourites:

☆ Squash-rackets

This is the old-fashioned name for squash. It's a bit like playing tennis inside a house. With smaller rackets. And a smaller ball.

☆ Eton-fives

This is a handball game that's played in a three-sided court by two teams of two players. The object of the game is to whack a small, hard ball around the court. To be a top player, you have to be lightning quick. Luckily, Roald Dahl was.

☆ Rugby

Roald Dahl called this rugger. A rugby ball is that odd shape because it used to be made from a pig's bladder. When the bladder was puffed full of air – not a popular job – it formed an oval shape rather than a perfect sphere. Nowadays rugby balls are made from rubber. Pigs everywhere heave a sigh of relief!

True or false?

When he was at boarding school, and during the winter months, it was Roald's job to warm up a lavatory seat for the house prefect – by sitting on it.

True

The toilets were inside an unheated outhouse, which meant that they were very cold in winter. Sometimes, Roald had to wipe frost off the seat before he sat down. He always made sure he took a good book to read, though.

A new medicine

'So-ho! thought George suddenly. *Ah-ha!* *Ho-hum!* I know exactly what I'll do. I shall make her a *new* medicine, one that is so strong and so fierce and so fantastic it will either cure her completely or blow off the top of her head. I'll make her a *magic medicine*, a medicine no doctor in the world has ever made before.'

Real marvellous medicines

In 1798, English doctor Edward Jenner discovered that if he injected the fluid from cowpox blisters into the skin of healthy people they were immunized against the deadly smallpox virus. He had discovered the very first vaccine.

American dentist William Morton was credited with the first successful use of **anaesthetic** during an operation in 1846. However, Crawford Long – an American surgeon – had been using anaesthetic since 1842.

English surgeon and scientist Joseph Lister discovered that it was vitally important to keep operation wounds absolutely clean to avoid infection. He first used antiseptic to clean wounds and surgeons' hands in 1865.

In 1902, Polish-born French physicist Marie Curie isolated the chemical element **radium**, which was used to treat cancer.

In 1928, Scottish bacteriologist Alexander Fleming discovered the antibiotic **called penicillin in a mouldy old dish in his lab. It is now used to treat infection and disease. Fleming won the Nobel Prize for his marvellous medical breakthrough.**

Q: Where did James, Old-Green-Grasshopper, Spider, Ladybird, Silkworm, Centipede, Earthworm and Glow-Worm play football?

A: On a giant football peach.

Q: What do you say to Mr Twit when he has stale bread, baked beans and smelly sardines poking out of his ears?

A: Anything you like – he can't hear you.

Q: What do you call a very clever girl who's an expert ballroom dancer?

A: Waltzing Matilda.

February

St Peter's
Weston-super-mare.
Feb 17th 1925

Dear Baby
        We had pancakes yesterday
because it was (pancake day) and
the cook took from 10 o'clock to half
dinner time to make pancakes for
all of us, because every one had
to be made separately, but they were
very nice, the cook said to Mr Frances
he was glad pancake day was not
every day. Give my love
to everyone. Love from

BOY

See
page
54

How to make pancakes

Pancake Day, also known as Shrove Tuesday, usually takes place this month. Here's how to make them – **but ask an adult to help as cooking can be dangerous.**

What you will need:

They're flipping good!

☆ 140g plain flour
☆ 284ml milk*
☆ 1 egg
☆ A bowl
☆ A whisk or a blender
☆ A non-stick frying pan
☆ A spatula
☆ A handy adult

* If you want to make orange-flavoured pancakes, squeeze the juice out of two oranges and add enough milk to make 284ml of liquid. Then make the pancakes exactly the same way. To make them really tasty, add a splash of orange juice and a drizzle of chocolate sauce when they're done. Mmm …

What you do:

1. Put all the ingredients in a bowl and whisk them together to make a sloppy batter. (If you have a blender, whizz the ingredients in one of these instead.)

2. Heat the frying pan on the hob, adding a knob of butter when it's hot.

3. When the frying pan is smoking hot, pour in half a cup of batter and quickly swirl it around.

4. Wait a few seconds, then loosen the edges with a spatula and shake the frying pan to make sure that the pancake doesn't stick.

5. After about a minute, FLIP the pancake up and over. Or turn it over with a spatula (you're more likely to end up with the pancake in the frying pan, but less likely to impress an audience).

6. When the pancake has cooked on the other side, eat with freshly squeezed lemon and a sprinkling of sugar.

Roald Dahl films

Do you know which of Roald Dahl's books have been made into films? Here's a list:

Willy Wonka and the Chocolate Factory

(1971) – starring Gene Wilder

The BFG

(1989) – with voices by David Jason, Amanda Root and Angela Thorne

Danny the Champion of the World

(1989, made for TV) – starring Jeremy Irons, Robbie Coltrane, Michael Hordern and Lionel Jeffries

The Witches

(1990) – starring Angelica Huston, Mai Zetterling and Rowan Atkinson

James and the Giant Peach

(1996) – with voices by
Simon Callow, Richard Dreyfuss,
Joanna Lumley
and Susan Sarandon

Matilda

(1996) – starring Mara Wilson,
Danny DeVito and Pam Ferris

Charlie and the Chocolate Factory

(2005) – starring Johnny Depp,
Freddy Highmore and
Helena Bonham Carter

Fantastic Mr Fox

(2009) – with voices by
George Clooney, Meryl Streep
and Bill Murray

Did you know?

Roald Dahl co-wrote the screenplays for the
James Bond film *You Only Live Twice* (1967)
and *Chitty Chitty Bang Bang* (1968).

Roald Dahl says...

'I have always regarded the mole as a friend because he eats all the horrid centipedes and leatherjackets and other pests that damage our flowers and vegetables . . . But I will tell you a very simple method of persuading a mole to leave your garden or your field. Moles cannot stand noise of any sort. It makes them even more nervous than they already are. So when I see a molehill in the garden, I get an empty wine bottle (plenty of those around in our house) and I bury it in the ground close to the molehill, leaving only the neck of the bottle sticking up. Now when the wind blows across the open top of the bottle it makes a soft humming sound. This goes on all day and night because there is almost always some sort of a breeze blowing. The constant noise just above his tunnel drives the mole half crazy and he very soon packs up and goes somewhere else. This is not a joke. It really works. I have done it often.'

True or false?

Only female mosquitoes bite people.

True

Goodness knows why. They just do.

Did you know?

A mole can dig approximately a metre of tunnel in an hour.

Valentine's Day

14 February is St Valentine's Day – officially the most romantic day of the year since the fourteenth century. However, it was not until the mid-nineteeth century that Valentine cards began to be popular, a craze begun by Esther Howland in the USA. Now approximately one billion Valentine's cards are sent every year.

Big Friendly Giants

The BFG had something in common with Roald Dahl. He was incredibly tall. Roald Dahl himself measured 1.98 metres (6 feet 6 inches). Here are more big friendly giants:

Robert Wadlow
(tallest man ever)
2.72 metres

Sultan Kösen
(tallest living man)
2.51 metres

Peter Mayhew
(Chewbacca of *Star Wars*)
2.21 metres

Michael Crichton
(author of *Jurassic Park*)
2.06 metres

Dave Prowse
(Darth Vader of *Star Wars*)
2.01 metres

Peter the Great
(Russian king)
2.01 metres

Christopher Lee
(Saruman in
Lord of the Rings)
1.96 metres

John Cleese
(actor and comedian)
1.95 metres

March

St Peter's

Weston-super-mare.

March. 24th 1926.

Dear Else

I will soon be coming home,
I am coming by train next Wedensday.
There is a craze for darts and
gliders, nearly every one has got
one, I hare got one (topping) one,
it glides like anythig, a boy
called Huntly-Wood made it for
me.

See
page
62

Top word

When Roald Dahl was a boy, *topping* did not mean something that you put on top of a cake or ice cream. It meant 'cool'.

How frightfully topping!

Unexpected happenings

Roald Dahl's *Tales of the Unexpected* were first shown on television in March 1979. These were eerie, ghoulish and very inventive stories with unexpected twists. The programmes were very successful in the UK and the USA.

Good weather for flying kites

March is traditionally a very windy month – perfect for flying kites! Here are some kite facts:

1. Kites first became popular in China, 3,000 years ago.

2. American inventor Benjamin Franklin proved that lightning was a natural phenomenon by flying a kite during a storm.

3. Wilbur and Orville Wright – the first people ever to fly – first tested their biplane designs as kites.

4. Kites have been used to ward off evil, deliver messages, spy, send radio signals and drop leaflets. They've even been flown for fun!

5. Kite-surfing is an exhilarating sport that uses a kite and a surfboard to send the kite-surfer whizzing from wave to wave across the sea.

What's the meaning of 'Roald'?

Roald is an Old Norse word that means 'famous'.

Other famous Roalds

Roald Amundsen was a famous Norwegian explorer who took part in one of the most exciting and dangerous races of all time. In 1911, he and Captain Scott – a British explorer – competed against one another to cross the treacherous Antarctic ice in an effort to become the first person to reach the South Pole. Amundsen won, possibly because of the extra spurts of energy provided by his delicious chocolate rations. Harald and Sophie Magdalene Dahl were so impressed by his record-breaking exploits that they named their son after him.

Roald is a small village in Giske, Norway. It is very famous indeed to the 700 people who live there, but Roald Dahl was never one of them.

All Over the World

Roald Dahl's books have been translated into **over 40 different languages** and are sold around the world.

Can you recognize the following titles?

1. Charlie und die Schokoladenfabrik (German)

2. Le Bon Gros Géant (French)

3. Danny El Campeon Del Mundo (Spanish)

4. Le Doigt Magique (French)

5. Los Cretinos (Spanish)

6. Das Wundermittel (German)

7. Agu Trot (Spanish)

8. Sophiechen und der Riese (German)

9. Charlie Y El Gran Ascensor De Cristal (Spanish)

10. Les Deux Gredins (French)

11. La Jirafa, El Pelicano Y El Mono (Spanish)

Answers on page 118

Did you know?

Roald Dahl's favourite composer was Beethoven. Here are a few more musical facts:

☆ **When** Beethoven **went deaf, he cut off the legs of his piano, so he could feel the vibrations in the floor when he played.**

☆ **The 17th-century French composer** Jean-Baptiste Lully **died when he stuck the spiked wooden staff he used to beat time into his foot instead of into the floor. The injury was mistreated, gangrene set in and he died from the infection.**

☆ **The 18th-century Italian composer** Rossini **loved eating more than he liked composing. He once wrote that he had only cried three times in his life: when his first opera was a flop, when he heard Paganini play the violin and the day a turkey stuffed with truffles fell overboard on a floating picnic.**

☆ **The 19th-century French composer** Hector Berlioz **was in love with two women. They both jilted him, so he decided to murder them. He disguised himself as a lady's maid, and set off from Rome to Paris with two double-barrelled pistols and various poisons. When he arrived in Nice, he got bored with his plan and had a delicious lunch instead.**

☆ **The 20th-century composer** Anton Webern **was accidentally shot by an American soldier in 1945 when he stepped outside to light an after-dinner cigar.**

Did you know?

The most expensive food in the world is harvested from the purple crocus, which begins to bloom in March. Saffron is made from the dried orange-red stigmas from inside the flowers and is used to turn rice and cakes bright yellow – as well as giving them a deliciously subtle flavour. But it comes at a price. A gram of saffron costs much more than a gram of chocolate, a gram of smoked salmon and even a gram of caviar.

AN INGENIOUS
(BUT TOTALLY ILLEGAL AND UTTERLY FORBIDDEN)
USE FOR SPRING LAMB

Spring lambs are born in March. And in his short story *Lamb to the Slaughter* Roald Dahl converts lamb into the most inventive murder weapon ever. A wife hits her husband over the head with a frozen leg of lamb, and then roasts the meat. The detectives who investigate the murder enjoy a slap-up meal – and eat the evidence!

April

APRIL FOOL

Gotcha!

This is an actual April Fool of a letter that Roald Dahl sent to his mother one year. He adored practical jokes.

April Fool

Why do we play April Fool jokes?

The custom may have begun in France when, in 1582, the calendar was adjusted to be more accurate. It meant that New Year's Day was moved from 25 March to 1 January. Anyone who continued to celebrate the end of the New Year week on 1 April was said to be a fool. An April Fool.

Fools beware!

**Play as many
April Fool jokes as you like
before noon
on 1 April, but remember that
those who play tricks *after* noon
become fools themselves.**

6 of the best April Fool jokes ever

1. When a television programme shown in 1957 fooled viewers into thinking that spaghetti grew on trees.

2. When an electronics expert convinced people in 1962 that they could turn their black-and-white televisions into colour televisions by stretching a pair of tights over the screen.

3. When a man set fire to a pile of tyres inside a dormant volcano in 1974. Black smoke belched into the air, fooling locals that Mount Edgecumbe was about to erupt. (Now that's bad!)

4. When astronomer Patrick Moore told radio listeners that the alignment of planets would create a temporary change in gravity and that if they jumped into the air at precisely 9.47 a.m. on 1 April 1976 they would experience weightlessness.

5. When a burger chain announced in 1998 that they were selling a left-handed burger, designed especially for left-handed people. Thousands flocked to buy them.

6. When in 2008 a television programme fooled viewers into believing that penguins flew thousands of miles to spend the winter basking in sunshine. See 'Flying Penguins' on **youtube.com**

Birdspotters, Watch out!

This is the month that flocks of birds return home after the winter. Look out for:

Skylarks

Greenfinches

Whitethroats

Willow warblers

Goldfinches

Golden plovers

Blackcaps

Swallows

House martins

Chiffchaffs

When is Easter Sunday?

Easter Sunday is usually in April, sometimes in March. It changes every single year. You can work out yourself when Easter Sunday will be using a calculator and a telescope (to check for full moons) . . . or you can simply consult this chart. Then you'll know when to look forward to all that lovely chocolate.

8 April 2012

31 March 2013

20 April 2014

5 April 2015

27 March 2016

16 April 2017

1 April 2018

21 April 2019

12 April 2020

Roald Dahl says...

'There is something incredibly exciting in finding a chocolate egg wrapped in silver paper cunningly hidden in the tuft of the heather plant or in the branches of ivy or in the bole of a hollow tree.'

5 golden rules for Organizing an Easter-egg hunt

START

1 Pick your hunting ground carefully – somewhere only you and your friends are going to be.

2 Get yourself a big bag of little chocolate eggs. (And remember ... there's no such thing as *too many* eggs.)

3 Make doubly sure there is no one around when you hide the eggs (very important, this, otherwise your hunt will be very brief).

4 Pick a variety of hiding places for the eggs – some high, some low, some cleverly hidden, some blindingly obvious. (This is a sure-fire way of making sure everyone finds some eggs.)

5 All eggs must be hidden by nightfall on Easter Saturday, ready for early risers the next day!

Or better still – get someone else to organize an Easter-egg hunt and then search for the chocolate eggs yourself.

75

What is Chocolate?

It's lovely, that's what it is. Oh, you mean what *is* it? Well . . . chocolate is a wonderful substance made from roasted and ground cacao seeds, usually sweetened and eaten as confectionery. **It's truly gloriumptious.**

A brief history of chocolate

☆ **6th century AD**
Chocolate was made by the Mayans in Central America from the seed of the cacahuaquchtl tree. The word 'chocolate' comes from their word 'xocoatl', which means 'bitter water'.

☆ **13th century**
The Aztecs used cocoa to make thick, cold chocolate drinks. Sugar was unknown, so they used different spices to flavour the drinks, including hot chilli peppers!

☆ **16th century**
Chocolate was brought to Spain by Hernando Cortez. The Spaniards mixed the beans with sugar, vanilla, nutmeg, cloves and other spices. Suddenly, it was a whole lot tastier. Spain managed to keep chocolate a secret from the rest of the world for almost 100 years.

☆ 17th century

Chocolate became popular in France, especially in the extravagant royal court of Louis XIV. It also reached Italy.

☆ 1657

London's very first chocolate shop opened, followed by many more. They became popular places for fashionable people to meet and chat and drink chocolate.

☆ 1711

Chocolate reached Austria . . .

☆ 1720

. . . and spread to Germany and Switzerland.

☆ 1755

America discovered chocolate. The first US factory opened ten years later.

☆ 1830

The very first chocolate confectionery was created by J. S. Fry & Sons, in Britain.

☆ 1849

The Cadbury brothers exhibited their chocolate in Birmingham.

☆ 1875

Daniel Peter, from Switzerland, produced the first milk chocolate bar.

☆ 1876

The rest is chocolate history.

The Queen's birthday

Her Majesty Queen Elizabeth II
was born on 21 April 1926. But she doesn't
just celebrate her birthday in April. Oh no.
She has more than one. How? See page 88.

May

May 9th 1926.

St Peter's
Weston-super-mare.

Dear Mama

Thank you for the Music Book and the
envelopes. I have played cricket twice this term,
and in the middle it began to rain but not
very hard so we were able to go on. On Monday
and Tuesday we were aloud to go down to the town
or sail our boats in the paddling pool on
the sands, or go on the pier, so we had quite
a nice time. The swiming baths ar'nt filled
yet, but they will soon be filled so we
can bathe.

Love from

B o y

See
page
98

See page 84

Roald Dahl says...

Back at school after the Easter holidays, young Roald used to rely on his trusty tuck-box to remind him of home. 'A tuck-box is a small pinewood trunk which is very strongly made, and no boy has ever gone as a boarder to an English prep school without one. It is his own secret storehouse, as secret as a lady's handbag, and there is an unwritten law that no other boy, no teacher, not even the headmaster himself has the right to pry into the contents of your tuck-box.'

In Roald Dahl's tuck-box

- ☆ Half a home-made currant cake
- ☆ A packet of squashed-fly biscuits
- ☆ A couple of oranges
- ☆ A pot of strawberry jam or Marmite
- ☆ A bar of chocolate
- ☆ A bag of Liquorice Allsorts
- ☆ A magnet
- ☆ A pocketknife
- ☆ A compass
- ☆ A box of conjuring tricks
- ☆ A catapult
- ☆ A couple of stink bombs

Whose lunchbox?

Can you guess which of Roald Dahl's characters might have owned these rather strange lunchboxes?

☆ Stilton cheese

☆ Tinned sardines

☆ Cornflakes

Mmm, tasty!

☆ Minced chicken livers

☆ Worms with a luscious tomato and cheese sauce

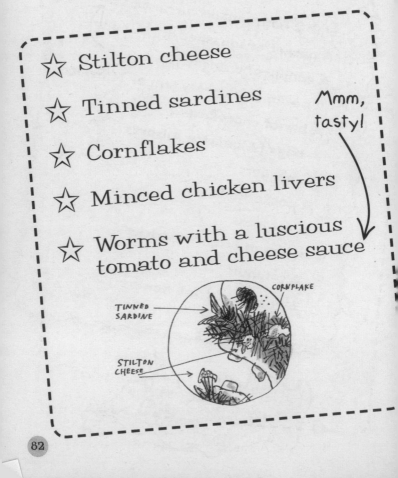

CORNFLAKE

TINNED SARDINE

STILTON CHEESE

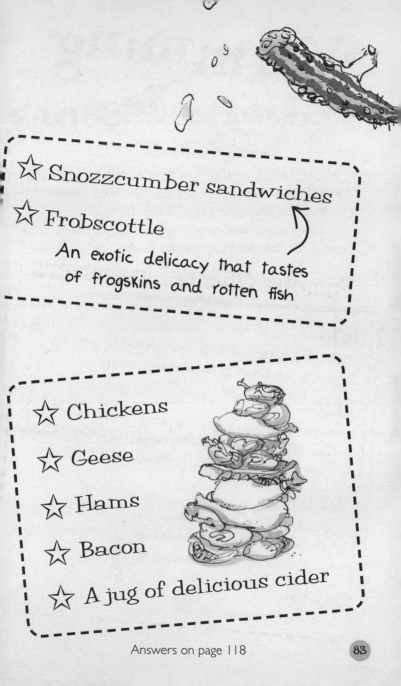

☆ Snozzcumber sandwiches

☆ Frobscottle

An exotic delicacy that tastes
of frogskins and rotten fish

☆ Chickens

☆ Geese

☆ Hams

☆ Bacon

☆ A jug of delicious cider

Answers on page 118

Swimming lessons

In the month of May, the pool at Roald Dahl's school was refilled with water. But not heated. Still, he learnt to swim when he was nine years old (and probably had to, so that he didn't freeze to death!).

Famous Channel swimmers

1875

Matthew Webb became the first person ever to swim the English Channel. It took 21 hours and 45 minutes.

1926

Gertrude Ederle became the first woman to swim the Channel. She beat the existing men's record by two hours with a time of 14 hours and 31 minutes.

1972

Lynne Cox became the youngest person to swim the Channel, beating both the men's and women's records with a time of 9 hours and 57 minutes. She was just 15 years old.

2006

David Walliams became the first comedian to swim the Channel with a time of 10 hours and 34 minutes, in aid of the charity Sports Relief.

True or false?

Roald Dahl was an RAF fighter pilot who carried out daring raids during the Second World War.

True

You can read all about his amazing adventures in *Going Solo*.

Flying machines

Here are some of the amazing
aircraft that Roald Dahl flew:

Hawker Hart
A plane with more oomph,
and deadly machine guns
on the wings.

Tiger Moth
Roald Dahl was so tall
his head stuck out of
the cockpit.

Hurricane
Powerful, speedy, tricky
and so little room in the cockpit
that Roald Dahl's knees almost
touched his chin.

Gladiator
A plane that fired
bullets *through* its
spinning propeller!

June

See
page
84

June 20ᵗʰ. 1926.

St Peter's

Weston-super-mare.

Dear Mama

Thank you for the cricket ball
and the choclate you sent me, it is
exacly the kind I wanted.
I have (swum) two lengths so far
and have not tried any more
but I could do more. I can very
nearly dive propely now, I hit the bottom
but I had my hands infront of me so
I did not hurt my self in fact I rather
liked it, I have nearly swum the bredth
under water. I am sending you my half
term (report).

See page 100

Love from

Roald.

The Queen's birthday

↳ again

Queen Elizabeth II has not one but *two* birthdays. Her real birthday is 21 April, but she has an official birthday* sometime in June or May or September, depending on where you are in the world. In the UK, her official birthday is the second Saturday in June, in New Zealand it's the first Monday in June and in most of Australia it's the second Monday in June, while in Canada it's the Monday on or before 24 May. In Western Australia, it's celebrated on the last Monday of September or the first Monday of October. If the Queen organized her diary really well, she could go to six of her own birthday parties every year!

---

* This tradition began when Edward VII – the Queen's great-grandfather – decided that it was a bit dull having a birthday in November and that it would be much nicer to celebrate when the weather was warmer and sunnier. And he was king. So he did.

Royal Star

The Queen is one of the very few real people who have starred in one of Roald Dahl's books. Give yourself a right royal pat on the back if you remembered that this book was *The BFG*.

Monarchs

since the Norman Conquest in 1066 and the dates of their reigns:

House of Normandy

1066–1087 William I
1087–1100 William II
1100–1135 Henry I
1135–1154 Stephen

House of Plantagenet

1154–1189 Henry II
1189–1199 Richard I
1199–1216 John
1216–1272 Henry III
1272–1307 Edward I
1307–1327 Edward II
1327–1377 Edward III
1377–1399 Richard II

House of Lancaster

1399–1413 Henry IV
1413–1422 Henry V
1422–1461 Henry VI

House of Yor

1461–1483 Edward
1483   Edward
1483–1485 Richard

House of Tudo

1485–1509 Henry VII
1509–1547 Henry VIII
1547–1553 Edward VI
1553–1558 Mary I
1558–1603 Elizabeth I

House of Stuart

1603–1625 James I
1625–1649 Charles I

Period of Interregnum

1649–1653 Commonwealth/
protectorate

1653–1658 Protectorate of
Oliver Cromwell

1658–1659 Protectorate of
Richard Cromwell

House of Stuart restored

1660–1685 Charles II
1685–1688 James II
1689–1694 William III and
Mary II (jointly)

1694–1702 William III
(sole ruler)

1702–1714 Anne

House of Hanover

1714–1727 George I
1727–1760 George II
1760–1820 George III
1820–1830 George IV
1830–1837 William IV
1837–1901 Victoria

House of Saxe-Coburg-Gotha

1901–1910 Edward VII

House of Windsor

1910–1936 George V
(Saxe-Coburg-Gotha until 1917)

1936 Edward VIII

1936–1952 George VI

1952– Elizabeth II

Backwards
and forwards

A palindrome is a word, phrase or sentence that says exactly the same thing, whether you read it front to back or back to front. Check out this list and then see if you can think of your own . . .

MUM

DAD

NOON

RADAR

DON'T NOD

EVIL OLIVE

DR AWKWARD

KAYAK

MADAM, I'M ADAM

TOO HOT TO HOOT

WAS IT A CAT I SAW?

Exam time

Find out if you're a clever clogs Matilda or just a Twit . . .

1. What did Matilda's wheeler-dealer dad do for a living?

2. Can you name James Henry Trotter's nasty aunts?

3. Did Roald Dahl like beards?

4. Who starred as Willy Wonka in the film version of *Charlie and the Chocolate Factory* (2005)?

5. Who were Farmer Boggis, Farmer Bunce and Farmer Bean?

6. How many Golden Tickets does Willy Wonka hide inside chocolate-bar wrappers?

7. What's the name of the little boy who tells the story of *The Witches*?

8. Which of the following grandparents did not belong to Charlie Bucket?
   a) Grandpa Joe
   b) Grandma Jolene
   c) Grandpa George
   d) Grandma Georgina

9. What do the initials BFG stand for?

10. What are tough and chewy and nasty and bitter?

Answers on page 119

Roald Dahl says...

'During this month the tadpoles in the ponds are beginning to sprout tiny arms and legs, and soon they will be turning into small frogs. Be nice to frogs, by the way. They are your friends in the garden. They eat the beastly slugs and never harm your flowers.'

Q: What's a frog's favourite drink?

A: *Croaka-Cola.*

Frog facts

1. There are around 5,000 different types of frogs worldwide.

2. Frogs have poisonous skin glands.

3. Female frogs lay between a few hundred and a few thousand eggs – they take just a few days to hatch.

4. Only male frogs croak. Some kinds of frogs inflate their throats to sound louder. They can inflate their throats so much that they're larger than their heads!

5. Small frogs live on average for just one year. Large frogs live longer.

6. The smallest frog in the world is the Gold Frog from Brazil. It's only 10mm long!

7. All frogs eat other animals, usually insects. None eat plants.

Wimbledon fortnight

The All England Lawn Tennis Club

hosts the Wimbledon Championships during the last week of June and the first week of July every year. It's one of the four Grand Slam tournaments (so called because they're very important) held throughout the year. The others are the **Australian Open** (Melbourne, January), the **French Open** (Paris, June) and the **US Open** (New York City, September). If a tennis player or a doubles team holds all four titles at the same time, they have achieved the elusive **Grand Slam**.

These players actually did it:

☆ **Martina Navratilova (1983-4)**

☆ **Steffi Graf (1988, 1993-4)**

☆ **Serena Williams (2002-3)**

July

St. PETER'S
Weston-s-mare. See
98

July. 15th 1928.

Dear Mama
Thanks for your letter. Its been fearfully hot the last few days, and so please excuse writing because, having been to church, we've had to change hastily an into cricket shirt only, so my hand is rather shakey.

Last Wednesday we played the Parish church choir boys, with rather a flabby team, because we beat them so hollow last time.

Yesterday we had some swiming sports, the 4 lengths open, I won my heat, and hope to come 2nd in the final.

By the way, I'm coming home by the 12.25 no the 12.32, it arrives at Paddington at 4.5.

Love

Roald

See
page
84

97

The Ashes

This famous – but very tiny – trophy is said to contain a burnt bail. It symbolizes the ashes of English cricket after Australia defeated the English team in 1882. Ever since, the two countries have battled against each other in the Ashes Test Series. Australia has won the series more times (31 times compared to England's 30 wins). England is the current holder after winning the tournament in 2009 and again in 2011.

Cricket speak

Some expressions used by cricket commentators need a bit of explanation:

Baggy green – the hat worn by Australian players, so called because it is baggy and green

Bails – the two tiny pieces of wood that sit precariously on top of the stumps

Crumble – how the pitch is described when it's especially rough and pitted

Duck – a score of zero

Follow on – when the batting team are made to bat again, as soon as they are bowled out

Googly – a delivery by a right-arm spin-bowler, which a right-handed batsman may think will spin one way, but in fact spins in the opposite direction

Grubber* – a ball that stays very low after bouncing

Jaffa – a ball that is bowled so well that it cannot be played

LBW – this stands for Leg Before Wicket, which means that the ball would have hit the stumps if the player's leg had not been in front of them

Over – when six balls have been bowled

Stumps – the three upright wooden sticks at either end of the pitch

Yorker – a ball that whizzes under the bat near the batsman's toes. Curiously, it's also known as a Sandshoe Crusher.

*The Grubber was also the name of the sweet shop in *The Giraffe and the Pelly and Me.*

School reports

Roald Dahl's school reports weren't always good, they weren't always bad, but they were always entertaining. Here's his report from 1930, when he was fourteen years old:

REPTON SCHOOL.
HALF TERM REPORT.

Christmas Term, 1930

Form Remove, C.   Boy's Name R. Dahl   Place for Half Term 19

Number in Form 22

English Subjects.		14	A persistent muddler, writing and saying the opposite of what he means. Fails to correct this by revision or thought. Has possibilities. A.H.O.
	Set	Place	
Latin. M.M-O.	3	16	
Greek Geography J.F.C. German	–	17	Very weak, especially in Composition.
		–	Weak, but may improve.
French.		19	Weak, for the same reasons as in English. A.H.O.
Mathematics.			
Science.			

Housemaster's Report. He probably finds his new form master a bit puzzling. But as long as he attends & tries, he will get on.

B.S., 26.

100

More school reports of the rich, famous and super-talented

'He will either become a millionaire or go to prison'

Richard Branson, multi-millionaire entrepreneur

'Hopeless. Certainly on the road to failure'

John Lennon, The Beatles

'A good science student, but rather mediocre in French'

Albert Einstein, Nobel-prize-winning physicist

'Does not quite understand the meaning of hard work'

Sir Winston Churchill, British Prime Minister during the Second World War

'He makes good cakes'

David Beckham, world-famous football player

Leaving school

In July 1934, Roald Dahl left school forever.
Can you guess which of the following
five jobs he *didn't* do?

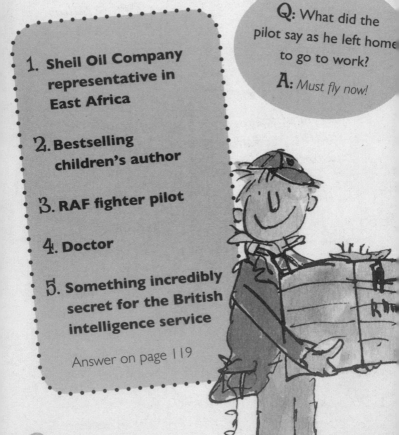

1. **Shell Oil Company representative in East Africa**

2. **Bestselling children's author**

3. **RAF fighter pilot**

4. **Doctor**

5. **Something incredibly secret for the British intelligence service**

Answer on page 119

Q: What did the pilot say as he left home to go to work?

A: *Must fly now!*

Now and then

These famous people didn't always do famous jobs.

	Now	Then
Harrison Ford	Actor	Carpenter
Brad Pitt	Actor	Delivering fridges
Jennifer Aniston	Actor	Waitress
Steven Spielberg	Director	Whitewashing fruit trees
Danny DeVito	Actor/Director	Hairdresser

True or false?
Roald Dahl rode a motorbike to school.

True

In his last summer term ever, Roald Dahl rode his beloved Ariel 500cc to a secret location near his school. (Motorbikes were quite forbidden – if he had been caught, he would have been expelled on the spot.) On Sunday afternoons, he would put on his disguise – waders, helmet, goggles and windproof jacket – and zoom around the countryside, right under the nose of his strict headteacher.

103

The best and worst * bits of
Norway

Roald Dahl went to Norway for his summer holidays every single year from the age of four to the age of seventeen. Here are his favourite bits:

1. **The celebration feast with his Norwegian relatives.**

2. **Krokaan – crisp burnt toffee bits that were mixed with ice cream.**

3. **The island of Tjöme – the greatest place on Earth, according to Roald.**

4. **The Hard Black Stinker – a battered old motorboat that Mrs Dahl used to ferry her children around the fjords.**

5. **Packing his ancient half-sister's boyfriend's pipe with goat's droppings instead of tobacco. The results were spectacular. (To find out more, read Boy.)**

*The worst bit was the sea journey from Newcastle to Oslo. Roald was horribly seasick all the way there. And all the way back.

Facts about Norway

Area:
385,199 sq km

Population:
4,920,000

Capital:
Oslo

Chief of State:
King Harald V

Biggest exports:
oil, natural gas and fish

Standard of living:
ranked number one in the world in 2011

Number of islands:
over 150,000

Most famous historical warrior inhabitants:
the Vikings (AD 800 to 1050)

Density of population:
16 people per square kilometre (in England, there are 402 people per square kilometre)

Daylight hours:
in northern Norway, the sun never sets between the middle of May and the middle of July. For two months in winter, it never rises.

Did you know?

A long-horned grasshopper doesn't have ears on the sides of its head. It has one on each side of its stomach. Weird? Then how about this: crickets' and katydids' ears are in their front legs, just below their knees.

Q: Where would you put an injured insect?

A: *An antambulance*

Q: What's a grasshopper's favourite game?

A: *Cricket*

August

A letter written by Roald in August 1934
– in the middle of the Atlantic Ocean!
He was seventeen.

R.M.S. NOVA SCOTIA.

FURNESS LINE

Thursday. At sea.

Dear Mama
This is Thursday, & we are due in at St. John's this afternoon at about 5 o'clock. We've had a marvellous voyage. Woke up on Saturday morning to find ourselves off the coast of Ireland. It looked a marvellous place. Later Scotland appeared on the other side & I took some photos of the Giants Causeway. After lunch, when we we left the coast of Ireland it started to blow & we didn't feel so good. However we remained on deck, and caught the wireless operator being sick over the side!

Globetrotting

At the beginning of August 1934, Roald Dahl went on his very first grown-up adventure. He and thirty other boys sailed to Newfoundland in Canada to take part in a backpacking expedition. Other marvellous and exotic places where Roald Dahl lived include:

☆ 1936–39 **Dar es Salaam, Tanzania**

☆ 1939–40 **Nairobi, Kenya**

☆ 1940 **Habbaniya, Iraq**

☆ 1940 **Ismailia, Egypt**

☆ 1940–41 **Alexandria, Egypt**

☆ 1941 **Elevsis (near Athens), Greece**

☆ 1941 **Haifa, Israel**

☆ 1942–45 **Washington DC, USA**

☆ 1948–60 **New York City, USA**

☆ 1960–90 **Great Missenden, Buckinghamshire, England**

Roald Dahl says...

'August is the month when baby adders are born in heathy, hilly places, and baby grass snakes emerge from their eggs in rotting leaves and old compost heaps.'

True or false?

Pemmican is mouth-watering Norwegian ice cream. Roald Dahl ate it non-stop during his summer holidays.

False

It's actually a high-protein snack made from pulverized meat, dried berries and fat. It's packed with energy, which makes it ideal for tough journeys, such as the long trek Roald Dahl once made through Newfoundland. Unfortunately, pemmican isn't as delicious as ice cream.

Star spotting

August is a splendid month to look out for stars in clear summer skies. And if you're lucky enough to be in the countryside, or on holiday somewhere remote, then they'll be even brighter. Here are some of the most famous constellations (a group of stars) in the northern hemisphere at this time of year:

The seven brightest stars are also known as the Big Dipper or the Plough.

Ursa Major

Cassiopeia

Cygnus

Draco

The North Star

Also called the Pole Star or Polaris, the North Star is the most famous star in the northern sky. It stays in the same place while all the other stars circle round it, so, for thousands of years, people have used it to help them find their way across sea and land (very handy if you get lost). You can always tell which way is north by looking at the North Star. If you stood at the North Pole, the North Star would be directly overhead.

To find the North Star in the sky, first find the Big Dipper and follow the two stars at the end of the basin upwards. This should lead you directly to the North Star.

Bored with the summer holidays?

Then learn Morse code and read the secret message below. (Each word is in brackets and there's a forward slash separating each letter.)

Morse code was used to send the first telegraph messages in the 1830s, before the telephone had been invented. The code is still used by radio amateurs around the world. The most famous Morse code message is the emergency signal **S-O-S**.

(. _/. . _/. . _/___ /._ ./. ./. ./. _/_ _ .) (_ / ___)

(. _/___ /. _/. _/. . ./. . .) (_ . ./. _/. . . ./. . _./. _ . . _)

(_ /. . . ./ .) (_ _/___ /. . ./ _) (_ /. . . ./. _ ./. . ./. . . ./.

_ . ./. . / _ ./ _ _ .) (_ / ___ /_ _ /. ./_ _/) (. . /_ .)

(. . . ./. . ./. . .) (. _ _/. . . ./___ /. _ . ./.)

(. _ . ./. . ./. _ ./.) (. _ _/. _/. . .) (_ . . ./. ./. . ./. _/_ _

(. . . ./___ / . _ ./ . _) (. _ . _ . _)

Answers on page 119

A	B	C	D	E
·_	_···	_·_·	_··	·

F	G	H	I	J
··_·	__·	····	··	·___

K	L	M	N	O
_·_	·_··	__	_·	___

P	Q	R	S	T
·__·	__·_	·_·	···	_

U	V	W	X	Y
··_	···_	·__	_··_	_·__

Z	.	?	-	,
__··	·_·_·_	··__··	_···_	·_·_·_

Did you know?

The true inventor of the Morse code as we know it today was not Mr Morse but his partner, Alfred Vail. Samuel Morse invented the original equipment and code for the electric telegraph, but the system had problems. Vail, who had agreed to build the system's hardware, was forced to create a completely new printing mechanism and a new code to make it work. This was the dashes-and-dots 'Morse' code, which has been used ever since.

Q: What's yellow, fuzzy and goes at 180 miles per hour?

A: A fuel-injected peach.

Q: What's very, very tall and goes 'tnaig drawkcab a'?

A: A giant talking backwards

Last words

Throughout his long life, Roald Dahl
lived by this inspiring verse, which
was written in 1920 by US poet,
Edna St Vincent Millay:

My candle burns at both ends
It will not last the night;
But ah, my foes, and oh, my friends –
It gives a lovely light.

More marvellous Roald Dahl reads

THE BFG (1982)

BOY: TALES OF CHILDHOOD (1984)

CHARLIE AND THE CHOCOLATE FACTORY (1964)

CHARLIE AND THE GREAT GLASS ELEVATOR (1973)

DANNY THE CHAMPION OF THE WORLD (1975)

GEORGE'S MARVELLOUS MEDICINE (1981)

GOING SOLO (1986)

JAMES AND THE GIANT PEACH (1961)

MATILDA (1988)

THE WITCHES (1983)

Collections

SONGS AND VERSE (2005)

THE ROALD DAHL TREASURY (2003)

Teenage fiction

THE GREAT AUTOMATIC GRAMMATIZATOR AND OTHER STORIES (1996)

SKIN AND OTHER STORIES (2000)

THE VICAR OF NIBBLESWICKE (1991)

THE WONDERFUL STORY OF HENRY SUGAR AND SIX MORE (1977)

For younger readers

THE ENORMOUS CROCODILE (1978)

ESIO TROT (1990)

FANTASTIC MR FOX (1970)

THE GIRAFFE AND THE PELLY AND ME (1985)

THE MAGIC FINGER (1966)

THE TWITS (1980)

Picture books

DIRTY BEASTS with Quentin Blake (1983)

THE ENORMOUS CROCODILE with Quentin Blake (1978)

THE GIRAFFE AND THE PELLY AND ME with Quentin Blake (1985)

THE MINPINS with Patrick Benson (1991)

REVOLTING RHYMES with Quentin Blake (1982)

Answers

The scrambled fireworks page 27

Roman candle, crack banger, fire serpent, rocket, golden rain.

New Year's resolutions page 44

1. Willy Wonka – it was never the same after the Great Glass Elevator made a quick exit . . .
2. Matilda.
3. James Henry Trotter.
4. Charlie Bucket.
5. Mr Twit – well, you'd do the same if you'd accidentally eaten worms, wouldn't you?

All over the world page 65

1. *Charlie and the Chocolate Factory.* 2. *The BFG.* 3. *Danny the Champion of the World.* 4. *The Magic Finger.* 5. *The Twits.*

6. *George's Marvellous Medicine.*

7. *Esio Trot.* 8. *The BFG.*

9. *Charlie and the Great Glass Elevator.*

10. *The Twits.*

11. *The Giraffe and the Pelly and Me.*

Whose lunchbox? pages 82–83

The Twits, the BFG, Fantastic Mr Fox.

Exam time page 93

1. He was a car dealer – and a rather dodgy one at that. 2. Aunt Spiker and Aunt Sponge. 3. Absolutely not. He *hated* hairy faces. If you don't believe me, read *The Twits*. 4. Johnny Depp. 5. They were the farmers who tried to outwit Fantastic Mr Fox. 6. Five. 7. Goodness knows! You can read *The Witches* from start to finish and back again, but you'll never find the answer. 8. b) Grandma Jolene, of course. Charlie's other grandmother was Grandma Josephine. 9. Big Friendly Giant. 10. Children. Or so says the Notsobig One in *The Enormous Crocodile*.

Leaving school page 102

4. Roald Dahl was never a doctor, although he secretly longed to be one. He did, however, help to invent a tiny medical valve for draining excess – and dangerous – fluid from the brains of sick children.

Morse code message
page 112

According to Roald Dahl the most thrilling moment in his whole life was being born.

There's more to
Roald Dahl
than great stories . . .

Did you know that 10% of author royalties* from this book go to help the work of the Roald Dahl charities?

Roald Dahl's Marvellous Children's Charity exists to make life better for seriously ill children because it believes that every child has the right to a marvellous life.

This marvellous charity helps thousands of children each year living with serious conditions of the blood and the brain – causes important to Roald Dahl in his lifetime – whether by providing nurses, equipment or toys for today's children in the UK, or helping tomorrow's children everywhere through pioneering research.

Can you do something marvellous to help others?
Find out how at **www.marvellouschildrenscharity.org**

The Roald Dahl Museum and Story Centre, based
in Great Missenden just outside London, is in the
Buckinghamshire village where Roald Dahl lived and
wrote. At the heart of the Museum, created to inspire a
love of reading and writing, is his unique archive of letters
and manuscripts. As well as two fun-packed biographical
galleries, the Museum boasts an interactive Story Centre.
It is a place for the family, teachers and their pupils to
explore the exciting world of creativity and literacy.

Find out more at **www.roalddahlmuseum.org**

Take a tour of Roald Dahl's
scrumdiddlyumptious
official website with your
favourite characters at

www.roalddahl.com

WINNER
BEST MUSICAL
EVENING STANDARD AWARDS

★★★★★

'A GLEEFULLY NASTY EVENING
OF UNADULTERATED BLISS'
GUARDIAN

Matilda

THE MUSICAL

BOOK
DENNIS KELLY

MUSIC & LYRICS
TIM MINCHIN

Based on the original story by ROALD DAHL, illustrated by QUENTIN BLAKE

CAMBRIDGE THEATRE
MATILDATHEMUSICAL.COM

WORLD
BOOK
DAY

1 MARCH 2012

Want to **WIN**
a year's supply of **BOOKS**
for you and your school?

Of course you do ...

This book is by one of our favourite authors (that's why it's in our **HALL OF FAME**!), but we want to know what *your* favourite book is (or *your* favourite character – whether it's the baddest baddie or the superest hero)!

It's that easy to win, so visit
WWW.WORLDBOOKDAY.COM now!